KATY TRAIL

A Guided Tour through History

Includes 9 Historic Rides

BY KATHY SCHRENK

FOREWORD BY DAN BURKHARDT

REEDY PRESS

DEDICATION

To Arlene and Chuck Young. They loved trails *and* rails. They gifted me my love for cycling. It's a habit that has always boosted my mood and eased me through some of my toughest moments. I miss them on every ride.

Reedy Press
PO Box 5131
St. Louis, MO 63139
www.reedypress.com

Cover design: Eric Marquard
Cover images: Main, Kathy Schrenk; Inset (l to r): The State Historical Society of Missouri, Kathy Schrenk, Dan Burkhardt, Kathy Schrenk, The State Historical Society of Missouri
Interior design: Eric Marquard

ISBN: 9781681063034

Printed in the United States
21 22 23 24 25 5 4 3 2 1

TABLE OF CONTENTS

MARTHASVILLE
FEED & SUPPLY CO.

TRELOAR-ON THE KATY SINCE 1896

MAGNIFICENTMISSOURI.ORG

ACKNOWLEDGMENTS

THIS BOOK would not have been possible without my husband, Nathan, and his willingness to hold down the fort and manage three kids' pandemic distance learning while I spent days riding.

Thanks to Josh Stevens at Reedy Press for the idea and the confidence in my ability. Julie McNamee and Barbara Northcott at Reedy Press deserve much thanks for their incredible attention to detail and commitment to making this book the best it could be.

Thanks to all who helped with research: Dianne Pankau, Frank Van Camp, Donna Nestle, Melanie Robinson-Smith, James Denny, Greg Harris, Lauren Sallwasser, and Wayne Lammers. Thanks to my writing and research buddies, Rachel, Molly, Jen, Kurt, Chappy, Ben, and David.

And big thanks to the rangers and everyone at the Missouri State Parks and Department of Natural Resources who keep the Katy safe and open to those who have traveled it over the years.

FOREWORD

IF THINGS GO AS PLANNED, ST. LOUISANS COULD PARK NEAR THE OLD KATY TRACKS AT ST. CHARLES, MOUNT THEIR BICYCLES, AND PEDAL TO SEDALIA ON THE WESTERN SIDE OF THE STATE . . . RIGHT NOW THIS IS ONLY A DREAM, SEVERAL YEARS FROM COMPLETION. MUCH MUST BE DONE BEFORE MISSOURIANS CAN HAVE ONE OF THE FINEST HIKING AND BIKING TRAILS IN THE COUNTRY.

– *ST. LOUIS POST-DISPATCH* EDITORIAL, MAY 26, 1986

I have been privileged to know about the Katy Trail since it was just a twinkle in Ted Jones's eye, before the *Post-Dispatch* wrote those words, before Missourians had heard the term "rail to trail." Thirty-five years later, Kathy Schrenk is taking you on a trip across Missouri, on a dream that came true, on what has become the "finest hiking and biking trail in the country."

The Katy Trail is something unique. It's a linear state park that runs almost completely across a big state. It's America's longest rail-to-trail pathway, following America's longest river, and it connects the backyards of Missouri's largest cities. One of those cities cheers for the blue of the Kansas City Royals, and the other knows only the red of the St. Louis Cardinals. The Katy Trail takes riders and walkers into places—under river bluffs, through old railroad towns, and past farm fields—few visitors had seen before the Katy was created.

The landscape the Katy passes has seen many changes since Daniel Boone hunted and lived here and Lewis and Clark followed this route west from St. Louis. It has been the home to native Americans, fur traders, German immigrants, steamboats, railroads, and farmers, all drawn here by the resources the Missouri River Valley offered. Many of the places that Kathy has captured here reflect that history and those changes. The Katy Trail is the most recent iteration of this centuries-old progression, yet another chapter in the life of this landscape.

In the 35 years since the Katy first became a possibility and the 30+ years since it became a reality, millions have visited the places that you'll read about here. Intrepid riders and walkers have traversed the entire trail, and some have ridden its length many times. Riding the Katy is indeed a "bucket list" item for cyclists from around the country and the world.

However most riders and walkers are more focused. They seek out pieces of the more than 280 miles of the trail to explore and sometimes return

PHOTO COURTESY OF DAN BURKHARDT

to those places again and again. But how to know where to begin on a pathway whose length would take you from Connecticut to Virginia? The way to get started is to find a guide who can show you how to experience this massive trail, one mile at a time. Thanks to Kathy, her bicycle, her historian's mind, and her photographer's eye, you have met the guide you seek! *Katy Trail: A Guided Tour Through History* shows us how to enjoy the trail whether we're looking for a five-day, end-to-end adventure or a half-day, out-and-back excursion a few minutes from home. The trail is a place where young and old, athletic or not, can ride or walk through the Missouri countryside.

The "dream" of the Katy Trail resulted from a case of pure and simple envy. Ted Jones, who had traveled the United States for his entire career, had seen it all—every nook and cranny and every side road and big city in America. But when he saw a new idea, a "rail to trail" project on a trip to Wisconsin in the mid-1980s, he was jealous. He wanted Missouri to have a trail like this, something that would allow visitors—as well as local residents—a way to experience the state he loved in a way that did not yet exist.

When you visit America's longest and narrowest state park, remember that you are experiencing the beauty of someone else's front yard, farm field, or forest. You'll see the eastern bluebird, Missouri's state bird, flitting down the trail ahead of you. You'll look out at giant pecan trees and oaks in the fence rows of the farm fields, smell the ripening corn crop in the fall, and visit towns that were built for the arrival of the Katy Railroad in 1896.

Daniel Boone, whose home is described in this book, was once asked if in all of his explorations he had ever been lost. Boone said, "I was never lost but I was once confused for several days." You will be neither lost nor confused with this book as your guide!

Dan Burkhardt
Magnificent Missouri

FALL COLORS
PHOTO COURTESY OF KATHY SCHRENK

INTRODUCTION

THE STORY of America is, in many ways, the story of its westward expansion. When many people who have never been to the United States thinks of this land, their first thought is often of cowboys, wagon trains, and gold miners rushing to the West. The inherent restlessness of the American story has shaped the land and the way its inhabitants relate to the land and to each other for centuries. For good or ill, it was always a foregone conclusion that Americans would move west until there was no more west to explore.

In ways big and small, the Katy Trail tells that story—one of an entire continent's history over the course of centuries—on a human scale.

The Missouri River was synonymous with westward expansion long before St. Louis declared itself the "Gateway to the West." It carried the Lewis and Clark expedition on the first parts of their journey, a warm-up for the dangers and thrills of the rugged mountains and wilds to come.

Explorers and traders in the river economy were inspired to create another of the great historic trails of America, the one to Santa Fe that opened trading with the Southwest and Mexico. The river guided the Donner Party and thousands of their fellows west toward Independence, Missouri, considered the "jumping-off point" for mid-19th-century immigrants hoping to settle in the sunny, verdant promised land of California.

Finally, after the Civil War, this corridor was key to the ultimate in overland migration: the railroads. The Missouri-Kansas-Texas Railway was formed as part of the US Pacific Railway in 1865. Commonly referred to as the MKT, then the KT, and then the Katy, it was part of a network of rail lines that drove the incredible growth of the postwar era and brought the coasts together into one nation.

Of course, change is as big a part of the history of our nation as anything. Interstate highways and passenger airlines ate into railroad companies' profits, forcing more and more to go out of business. But that isn't the end of the story. For many of these old railbeds, a new era has arrived. The ranchlands, river vistas, bluff views, and vineyards of Missouri are accessible to anyone willing to throw their leg over the saddle of their favorite bike. Thanks to the vision of a small group of dedicated trail boosters, the longest continuous bike trail in the country is right here. A ride through history, a journey of discovery, through a former state capital and the current one, and in the footsteps of Meriwether Lewis, William Clark, Daniel Boone, and countless other adventurers over the centuries.

Ride the Katy and it's all there, and not just the grand scope of history, but America in microcosm, including a small city adapting by converting an old factory into loft apartments; others facing natural disaster with a resilience that everyone in this changing world can learn from; and many parlaying some of the country's oldest grapevines into a booming tourism industry.

Ride the Katy for a two-wheeled adventure through time and place like no other.

THE KATY TRAIL: A RAILS-TO-TRAILS SUCCESS STORY

THE DECLINE of America's railroads began in earnest after World War II. Suddenly, everyone had a car and no longer wanted to travel based on someone else's schedule.

In the mid-1960s, folks started noticing that abandoned rail lines would make lovely walking and biking trails. The nascent movement grew slowly in the following decades, but, in 1983, Congress passed legislation to make it easier for rail companies and parks systems to work together to turn these spaces into trails. In 1986, there were 250 miles of rail-trails. Thirty years later, there were more than 21,000 miles of trails across the country.

The Katy Trail is the longest and one of the most successful rail-trail projects. But the path to this success wasn't always smooth, in part because the Missouri legislature wasn't always generous with funds for the trail's development. However, Ted Jones, son of the founder of Edward Jones, had discovered another rail-trail on a trip to Wisconsin in the 1980s and donated $200,000 to the cause. Ted Jones was the trail's biggest booster until his death in 1990.

Then, a group of landowners bordering the Katy right-of-way sued to stop trail development; some even physically blocked the trail with barriers.

But it wasn't long before cyclists came to the small towns along the trail and brought cash with them. Restaurants, shops, and inns sprouted like mushrooms, and the trail was popular with users and neighbors alike.

The outlook was rosy, and 67 miles of trail were open for all of two years when the infamous Great Flood of 1993 hit, halting construction and ruining much of the 125 miles of trail that had already been built. In memory of Ted, the Edward Jones company stepped in and helped fund reconstruction of the trail.

In 1996, 185 miles of Katy Trail State Park opened from St. Charles in the east to Sedalia in the west. The westernmost 40 miles opened between Sedalia and Clinton in 1999, and the final 12 miles from St. Charles to Machens opened in 2011.

Now, cyclists, walkers, and train buffs alike can explore more than 200 miles of trail over 20-plus steel truss bridges. They travel through towns that started as river ports and became railroad towns or found new life around wineries after Prohibition. They drink in the views of the farmlands, the rolling ranchlands, and the river bluffs that characterize central Missouri. Nothing like the Katy Trail exists anywhere in the country, nearly spanning the 21st-largest state and drawing cycle tourists from around the world.

HOW TO USE THIS BOOK

IT DOESN'T MATTER WHETHER IT'S RAINING OR THE SUN IS SHINING OR WHATEVER: AS LONG AS I'M RIDING A BIKE, I KNOW I'M THE LUCKIEST GUY IN THE WORLD.
                                              – MARK CAVENDISH, BRITISH PRO BIKE RACER

THIS GUIDE was written with any and all trail users in mind, from long-distance cyclists to casual day-riders to families looking for the occasional weekend outing with young riders. It's broken down into seven sections, five of which describe trails that and end at a town that has plenty of lodging and dining options. The "what to expect" bullet points at the start of each section give you an idea of how much to pack for your journey and what to prepare. The highlighted stops on each trip provide insights into historical locales and the history of a spot or region.

Every year, thousands of cyclists take overnight trips on the Katy, either staying at inns or bed-and-breakfasts on the way or "bikepacking," that is, carrying tent, sleeping bag, and everything else they need to stay out on the trail for days at a time. Thousands more leave a car at one end and drive with a friend to another trailhead to make it a long ride without doubling back.

Each section can be completed as one day trip or part of a multiday trip. Whether you park and do an out-and-back ride, organize a vehicle shuttle, or take Amtrak as your shuttle, this guide will give you a sense of the rich history of the region.

SAFETY FIRST

- Wear your helmet!

- Tell someone trustworthy (spouse, friend, coworker) where you're going and when you'll be back. Check in with them when you return. If you don't return in time, rescue workers will know where to look.

- Bring lots of water and snacks—more than you think you'll need.

- There are many areas of the trail where you won't have cell phone service. Bring equipment for changing a flat and making small adjustments in case you can't get help via phone.

- Respect the sun and heat—that means sunscreen, sunglasses, and, if your ride is longer than an hour, electrolyte drinks or tablets. Summers in Missouri can be dangerously hot and humid with the heat index regularly shooting above 100 degrees. Know the signs of heat exhaustion and heat stroke.

- Winter is a great time to get outdoors in Missouri. Daytime temperatures frequently poke above 50, and snow doesn't usually stay around long. Remember to wear layers, just as you would on a hike, run, or other winter outdoor activity. A thin synthetic beanie that fits under your helmet is an essential accessory. During winter, hydration is just as important as in summer, and it can be easy to forget to drink regularly when you're not sweating buckets. Remember that water fountains available in summer may be shut off in winter, so carry extra water. Sunscreen and eye protection should be worn in winter as well. The days are short, so pack a flashlight or headlamp just in case.

- The online Katy Trail State Park Advisory Map is a great resource for finding out about trail closures and sections of trail that might be rough or have a tree down.

LOGISTICS

THE KATY TRAIL is composed of crushed gravel throughout its 237 miles. It's mostly smooth and can be ridden with all kinds of bikes, with the exception of the racing equipment with delicate tires intended for smooth tracks or velodromes. The road, mountain, town, or hybrid bike that you regularly ride or that's been sitting in your garage, waiting to be dusted off and for you to buy a guidebook like this one, is a good fit for the Katy. When in doubt, have your local bike shop mechanic give your bike a safety check and tune-up.

Most long-distance cyclists with Katy experience consider west to east the ideal trip route. Most of the trail has a slight downhill grade toward the east, which is the direction the Missouri flows naturally. Cycling east also means favorable tail winds—usually.

MILE MARKERS

The Katy Trail mile markers don't always give an exact measurement of distance. This is because the state parks department has kept the historical railroad mile markers, and, in some cases, the trail deviates from the historic location of the railroad to route around obstacles or repairs.

SHUTTLES

Shuttle services provide a ride for a fee to allow trail users a point-to-point ride, instead of having to ride out and back. Following are some shuttle options:

- Bike Stop Café locations in St. Charles and Chesterfield provide shuttle service to Katy trailheads and Amtrak stations.
- Red Wheel Bike Shop in Jefferson City provides shuttles to and from the middle section of the Katy.
- Cab companies and other shuttle services are sometimes available for Katy riders. Check out www.bikekatytrail.com for the most up-to-date information on small businesses that provide shuttles.
- Amtrak trains can get riders from one end of the trail to another and act as a shuttle to eliminate the need to ride out and back. The Missouri River Runner train travels between St. Louis and Kansas City, and it stops in the following towns close to or on the Katy Trail: Washington, Hermann, Jefferson City, and Sedalia. Amtrak schedules change in response to demand, so check scheduling carefully before making plans.

CLINTON TO SEDALIA

SEDALIA

4

5

High Point
Elev. 955 feet

3

Rock Island Trail

2

WINDSOR

1

START!

CLINTON

RIDE 1

CLINTON TO SEDALIA
35.5 MILES

 ## WHAT TO EXPECT

- Clinton is the county seat of Henry County and has a number of hotels and services.
- The trail Ride from Calhoun to Windsor is almost totally shaded.
- Windsor has several restaurants and a grocery store.
- The Windsor to Green Ridge trail section has very little shade.

1 Clinton Courthouse Square
1.5 MILES FROM START OF KATY

The westernmost town on the Katy is, like most, an old railroad town. It benefited from the railroad but also managed to become mired in debt, thanks to the excessive issuance of railroad bonds. Built in 1893, this courthouse square is the largest in Missouri and, in October 1915, was the site of the Bond Burning Jubilee. Beginning in the 1860s, Clinton taxed its population to pay the bonds to the point where citizens compared the agony of the debt to the deprivations of Civil War days. When they finally paid off the debt, they had a party of epic proportions in which they burned 10 cords of wood to cook 500 pounds of beef, 100 pounds of mutton, 200 pounds of cabbage, and more. Today, the courthouse square looks like something out of a movie and is surrounded by restaurants, antique shops, and businesses of all kinds.

PHOTO COURTESY OF THE STATE HISTORICAL SOCIETY OF MISSOURI

? DID YOU KNOW?
Three Civil War skirmishes were fought in Clinton, and 10 times as many local soldiers fought for the Confederacy as the Union. A veterans' memorial at the courthouse square portrays a Union soldier standing next to a Confederate soldier.

DIRECTIONS
From the courthouse square, head north on Main Street for about three quarters of a mile, and then turn right on Sedalia until you reach the Katy trailhead after about half a mile. From here, it's about nine trail miles to Calhoun, where there is a bathroom and water at the trailhead, and then about seven miles to Windsor (mile marker 248).

② Rock Island Trail
MILE MARKER 247

The Rock Island Spur is the younger sibling to the Katy, and the trail's boosters hope that it will pair with the famous, older trail to make an epic loop of more than 300 miles. In 2019, the first 47 miles of the trail opened, from Windsor to Pleasant Hill, which is just outside Kansas City. If state parks succeed in raising the $8 million needed to develop the 144-mile segment east of Windsor, the Rock Island Trail would stretch all the way to Washington, MO, to complete the loop.

PHOTO COURTESY OF KATHY SCHRENK

The Rock Island rail line started in the 1850s in Chicago and eventually stretched south and west as far as New Mexico. The last train rolled off the Rock Island line in the 1980s.

DIRECTIONS
Head northeast on the trail from Windsor about five miles.

③ High Point
NEAR MILE MARKER 242

The highest point on the Katy Trail is 955 feet above sea level. This section between Clinton and Sedalia was added to the trail 10 years after the easternmost 162 miles and has a distinctive feel, home to gently rolling ranchland. The sound of a lowing cow is more likely to be heard than that of a farmer's combine. One can easily imagine the look of the plains rolling off toward Kansas and Oklahoma in the path of the rails as they were in the 1880s.

PHOTO COURTESY OF KATHY SCHRENK

DID YOU KNOW?
While this is the Katy high point, the Missouri state high point is in the Ozarks of southeast Missouri on rugged Taum Sauk Mountain at 1,772 feet above sea level.

DIRECTIONS
From the high point, ride northeast, past the Green Ridge trailhead at mile marker 239. Near mile marker 232, watch for a rail signal near a driveway on the right. It's on private property, but occasionally a rider will take that right by mistake and find that they have tripped a loud, clanging train crossing signal.

Sedalia Trailhead and Depot
MILE MARKER 228

At the east end of Sedalia, the historic train depot welcomes Katy Trail users and other tourists with its restored red brick and stone facade. Inside is a museum with rotating exhibits showing what life was like throughout the history of Sedalia before the Katy stopped running in the mid-20th century.

Today, one of Sedalia's claims to fame is the Scott Joplin Ragtime Festival. Joplin, one of American music's most influential composers, was born in Texas just after the Civil War to formerly enslaved people, and he spent much of his adult life in cities such as St. Louis and Chicago. But he spent part of his childhood and young adult years here, learning to play piano, attending college, and entertaining at social clubs for black men. It was in Sedalia that he wrote one of his most famous pieces, the "Maple Leaf Rag."

DIRECTIONS

From the depot, turn left onto E. 3rd Street, and then right on Mill. Mill turns into Main Street. After a quarter mile, turn right on Lamine Avenue and left on E. Pacific Street.

Lamy Building
.5 MILE FROM KATY

Across the street from the Amtrak station in Sedalia is a historic landmark that has been transformed into a blend of artful architecture and modern function that pays homage to the building's history. The Lamy Manufacturing Company was founded just after the end of the Civil War and moved into the three-story brick building on Pacific Street in 1893. The company made work apparel and became a primary local manufacturer of Levi's jeans after World War II. It was 1998 when the last pair of jeans was manufactured in Sedalia. Now, the beautifully restored building is home to restaurants, retail stores, offices, and apartments surrounding a soaring two-story entrance.

DID YOU KNOW?

The Daum Museum of Contemporary Art is on the campus of the State Fair Community College just a mile or so north of where the Katy passes the state fairgrounds. It's the kind of place you'd expect to find in a big city rather than a small, charming town surrounded by ranchland and cornfields. The museum hosts rotating exhibits alongside a permanent collection that features superstar artists from the past 50 years, including Andy Warhol, Ansel Adams, and Dale Chihuly.

FLORA AND FAUNA TO LOOK FOR

Native prairie grass, great horned owls, cattle

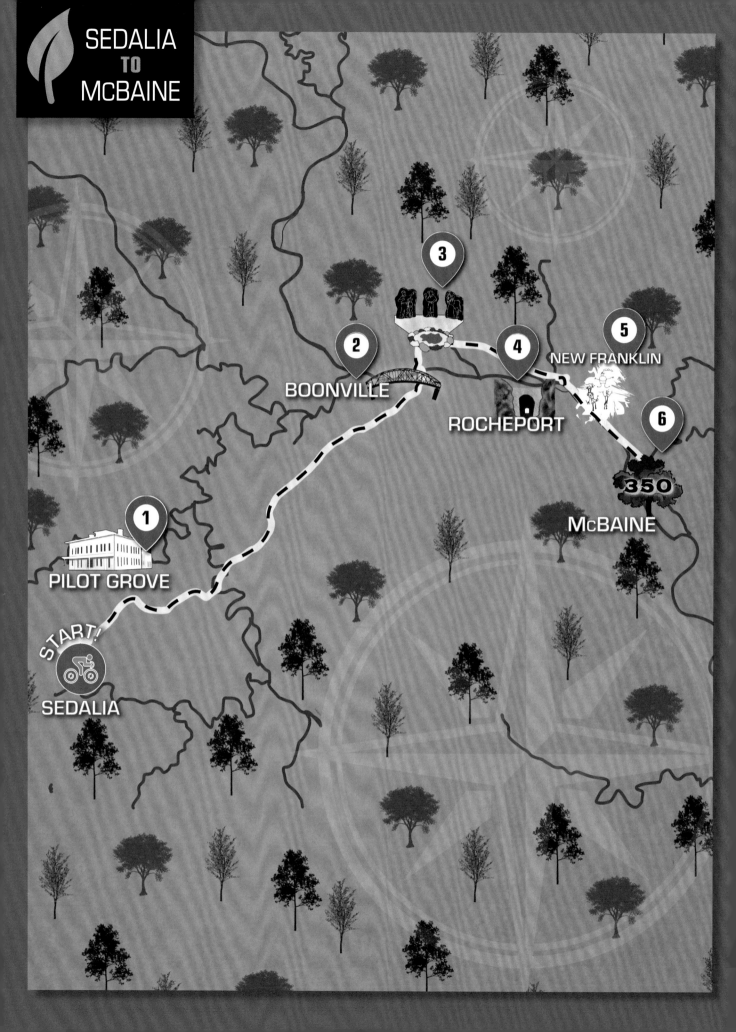

RIDE 2

SEDALIA TO McBAINE
COLUMBIA CONNECTION; 59.5 MILES

WHAT TO EXPECT

- A portion of the Katy through Sedalia reverted to private property, and a reroute was established in 2016 that requires riding on roads for about three miles.
- Boonville has many restaurants and lodging options.
- Another reroute on roads is necessary between New Franklin and Rocheport due to a washed-out bridge.
- Rocheport has camping, lodging, and restaurants.

DIRECTIONS

From the Lamy building in downtown Sedalia, return to the Katy Depot. Review the posted map for directions. There are some signs and directional arrows painted on the road. First, head east on 4th Street, and then turn left (north) on Engineer Avenue. Continue north, and, just past the Crown Hill Cemetery, turn right onto Reine Avenue. After a few blocks, the road changes names and becomes E. Griessen Road. By now, the setting is mostly rural so there isn't much traffic, but the road is narrow, so use caution and stay alert. The detour ends just past Randall Road, and a directional arrow painted on the road indicates the left turn.

Around mile marker 218, the trail passes between some low cliffs in one of the few places where the track builders had to blast away rock. Continue on the trail past the Clifton City trailhead (mile marker 215).

To see the Pleasant Green Plantation house, turn left from the trail onto Church Lane at mile marker 211, and go about half a mile. Turn left on Highway 135 to see the house immediately on your left.

PHOTO COURTESY OF KATHY SCHRENK

Pleasant Green Plantation House
.5 MILE FROM KATY

Pleasant Green Plantation is part of Missouri's "Little Dixie," a collection of extant antebellum houses in central Missouri. On some plantations, including this one, the slave quarters are still standing, providing a visceral reminder of Missouri's complicated past. This section of the state reaching from Kansas City east across the Missouri River was populated in the early 19th century by migrating southern farmers and planters who brought their agricultural and cultural practices with them. According to the 1840 census, 23 percent of Pilot Grove's population was enslaved.

Visitors can schedule tours, but even a viewing of the outside of the buildings provides a sense of the restored 1820 house and grounds. Built on a gentle rise, the property has views of the surrounding hills sloping down toward the Katy track and the nearby Johnson Branch of the Lamine River.

DIRECTIONS
Return to the trail and continue northeast past Pilot Grove, which has several spots to refuel, at mile marker 203 and Prairie Lick at mile marker 197.

PHOTO COURTESY OF RRP0423, WIKIPEDIA

2 The Boonville Bridge
MILE MARKER 192

After the westernmost 72 miles of trail, the Katy crosses the Missouri River. It doesn't veer far from the river's north bank the rest of its length, all the way past St. Charles.

Boonville is the furthest west of the many river towns on the Katy that transitioned to railroad towns during the 19th century. The bridge that allowed the KT line to cross the Missouri River was completed here in 1874 with a steam-powered swing span to accommodate river traffic and was considered an engineering marvel. It was replaced in 1932 with a vertical lift-span bridge that dominates the skyline and has captured the imagination of locals since it was revealed in 2004 that its owner, the Union Pacific Railroad Company, planned to dismantle it. Townspeople started a nonprofit and successfully lobbied Union Pacific to spare the bridge. They hope to restore the bridge to the point where it can connect the Katy Trail on both sides of the river, making it by far the longest dedicated Katy bridge and arguably the most spectacular for observers and riders. They still have millions of dollars to raise to make the plans a reality, and, for now, Katy users cross the Missouri River via a dedicated lane on the Highway 40 bridge.

DIRECTIONS

Follow the signs from the depot. The trail follows E. Morgan Street for one block before turning left onto a paved trail up the hill to Main Street, where it turns left and has a dedicated lane on the bridge over the Missouri River. Near mile marker 190.5, there's a Santa Fe Trail monument installed by the National Park Service. Continue 1.5 miles to Old Franklin and the Katy Roundhouse campground, and then another mile to New Franklin.

3 Santa Fe Trail Monument
MILE MARKER 188

PHOTO COURTESY OF KATHY SCHRENK

A group of stone monuments resembling pioneer figures surrounding an imaginary campfire greets visitors to the New Franklin trailhead. The trail originated here in September, 1821, when Franklin resident William Becknell left for New Mexico. Becknell arrived just in time to take advantage of newly independent Mexico and its hunger for trade in horses and mules. Franklin remained the eastern terminus of the famous trail for five years. After the town was flooded by the Missouri River twice in three years, it moved up the hill to where New Franklin is now.

? DID YOU KNOW?

While the Katy and Santa Fe Trails meet in Franklin, the Santa Fe veers north and west toward Independence, Missouri. The National Park Service maintains an auto tour route, and trail buffs can find ruts from the Santa Fe wagons still visible near the town of Marshall. Independence is home to the National Frontier Trails Museum, which has a wealth of information and exhibits about the three trails that used Independence as their jumping-off points: the Santa Fe, Oregon, and California Trails.

▸ DIRECTIONS

Near mile marker 181.4, watch for a narrow metal pedestrian bridge on the right. Go through the conservation parking lot, and turn left onto Highway 40. Go about three miles to the Highway 240 spur, and turn right. After about a mile, the highway turns into Central Street and leads through downtown Rocheport and to the Katy Trail.

4 Rocheport
MILE MARKER 178

Rocheport is one of the most picturesque towns on the Katy. Just west of the town is the only tunnel blasted for the train to go through. The town itself is loaded with adorable bed-and-breakfasts. There's a combination bike shop and cafe at the trailhead.

The hamlet was officially founded in 1825 but was mentioned in the writings of explorer Zebulon Pike in 1806. During the 1800s, it

PHOTO COURTESY OF KATHY SCHRENK

was the county's main river port, and its residents benefited from people coming from all around central Missouri to ship and receive goods.

Just east of the town on the Katy is a memorial to Edward (Ted) Jones, who used some of his financial services fortune to jump-start the Katy Trail in the 1980s, as mentioned earlier. In April 1990, this section between Rocheport and McBaine was the first to open to travelers.

5 Indigenous Drawings
MILE MARKER 177

PHOTO COURTESY OF KATHY SCHRENK

Just east of Rocheport, riders will find not only striking natural beauty but also visible evidence of the area's history. On the cliffs just outside town, watch for the MKT insignia carved into the rock. Above that, about 50 feet from the ground, are pictographs in the shapes of animals and humans, likely created by Sauk and Fox Indians, who lived here until around 1814. They were fist noted by white adventurers in 1819, but have faded considerably since then. The Indians likely used red pigment from iron ore to create these images.

Beyond these starkly beautiful drawings, there is little evidence or history of Missouri's first inhabitants to be found. There are no federally recognized tribes in the state today. When Lewis and Clark came through the area in 1804, the tribes had already been decimated by smallpox. The surviving Indians were forced west into what is now Oklahoma, Nebraska, and Kansas as a result of the Indian Removal Act of 1830.

DID YOU KNOW?
The name "Missouri" comes from a Sioux tribe and is thought to mean "one who has dug out canoes" or "town of the large canoes." Kickapoo, Osage, and Sioux are the tribes thought to have held the greatest influence on the land around the Katy Trail before Europeans ejected the natives who survived European-introduced diseases, warfare with other tribes, and battles with US government troops and immigrants.

DIRECTIONS
Continue east on the trail about nine miles. Turn right on Bur Oak Road. You'll see the big oak on your left.

6 Champion Bur Oak Tree
MILE MARKER 171

PHOTO COURTESY OF KATHY SCHRENK

Perhaps no other tree in the state inspires the devotion that this tree does. Generations of locals, as well as students at the nearby University of Missouri campus, have fond memories of visiting the tree with family members and classmates.

The tree is estimated to be at least 350 years old and was already big enough to be of note when the Lewis and Clark expedition passed through in 1804. It's the largest bur oak in the state and tied for the title of largest in the country with another bur oak in Kentucky.

The tree itself is roughly 90 feet tall, and its trunk is 23 feet around. It was struck by lightning and partially burned in October 2020, but as of this writing the mighty tree is healthy and standing strong.

DID YOU KNOW?
Return to the trail and travel east. Just past the bur oak and just before the McBaine trailhead is a nine-mile trail that connects the Katy to Columbia and the University of Missouri campus.

FLORA AND FAUNA TO LOOK FOR
Deer, opossum, armadillo, artist's conk

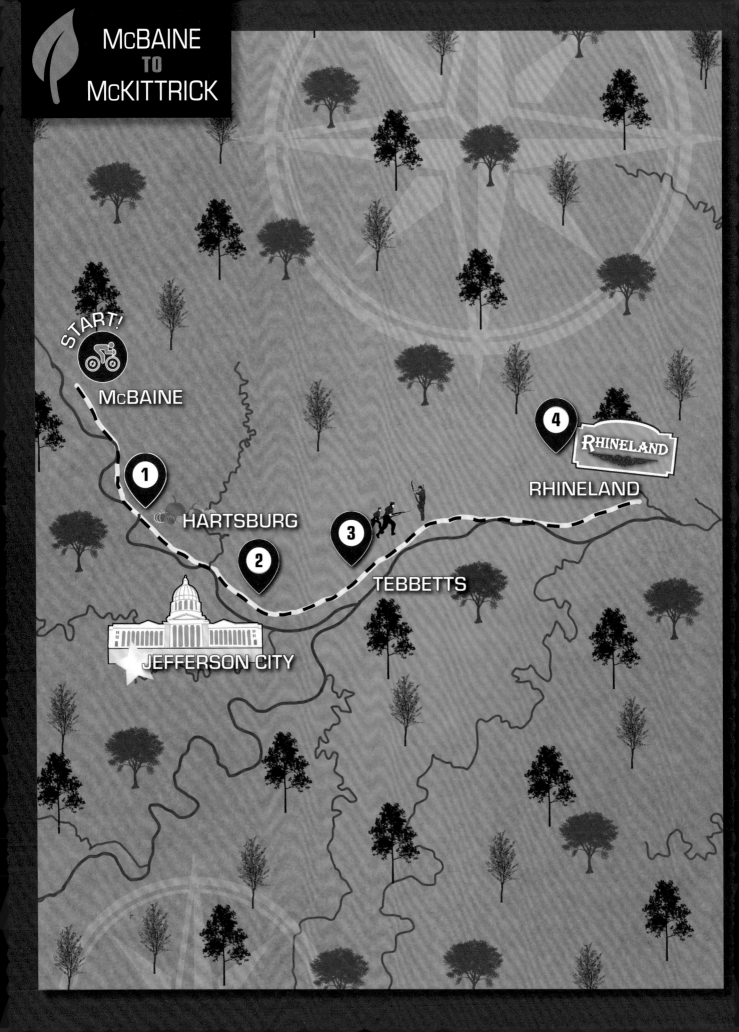

RIDE 3

McBAINE TO McKITTRICK

HERMANN CONNECTION; 68.5 MILES

🚴 WHAT TO EXPECT

- Camping is available in **Easley** (mile marker **162**) and **Hartsburg** (mile marker **153**).
- Be prepared to ride for almost **20** miles without potable water between the **North Jefferson** trailhead and **Mokane** (mile marker **125**).
- A trail closure from mile marker **116** to **118** will last at least until early **2022**.
  A severe rockslide that covered the trail in **2020** will require the transportation department to develop a plan to stabilize the cliff before parks workers can repair and reopen the trail. When a trail is closed, the parks department will often recommend an alternative route. In this case, however, there is no alternative route recommendation because Highway **94** is narrow and doesn't have a shoulder here. Riders should consult online or paper maps and use their judgment about how to safely get around the closure.
- **Mokane** and **Portland** are very small towns, but each has one restaurant/ bar as of this writing.
- **Bluffton** at mile marker **111** is a good place to camp and refuel. An honor-system refrigerator at Steamboat Junction has drinks and snacks, so be sure to have some small bills.
- After you head west from **Bluffton**, there's a stretch of a few miles that's mostly shadeless.
- **Rhineland** has several inns and a restaurant, if you want to stop before Hermann.

🧭 DIRECTIONS

From McBaine, head east on the Katy 16 miles. Near mile marker 166, watch for an interpretive sign with information on Roche Percee Natural Arch (aka Pierced Arch).

PHOTO COURTESY OF KATHY SCHRENK

① Hartsburg
MILE MARKER 153

Up to 50,000 people descend on this town with an official population of 108 souls every October. Hartsburg, also known as Missouri's Pumpkin Patch, hosts perhaps the largest pumpkin festival in Missouri, and the festival was just getting its start as some of the first Katy riders were rolling by in 1991.

Disaster struck the town in 1993 when the Great Flood damaged most of the buildings in the town and washed away the pumpkin plants that would produce the stars of the show. The town is also home to one of the best-preserved 1890s-era iron-and-frame storefronts, the Hackman Building, which is on the National Register of Historic Places.

PHOTO COURTESY OF JASON THOMAS

DID YOU KNOW?
The 1993 flood was the largest in the United States since 1927. Excess snowfall in the Dakotas and Minnesota the previous winter meant melting snow swelled the rivers come spring. When storms dumped record rainfalls across the Midwest, the ground was already saturated, and rain ran directly into the rivers instead of soaking into the soil. The Missouri River crested at 15 feet above flood level in the summer of 1993.

DIRECTIONS
At the N. Jefferson trailhead, take the spur trail south, following signs to Jefferson City and the pedestrian bridge. Turn right on 4th Street and left on Cottonwood Street. Pass under the vehicle bridge to access the Missouri River pedestrian/bike bridge, a series of ramps that allow cyclists and pedestrians to access the separated bridge lane and cross the Missouri River. Turn left on Main Street.

② State Capital
3 MILES FROM THE KATY

The plaza at the south end of the Jefferson City Bridge provides a commanding view of the capital city. At the other end of Main Street, relive your fourth-grade history field trip, or, if you're not a Missouri native, soak yourself in the history of the Cave State. Jefferson City has been Missouri's capital since 1826. The domed building that now houses the state offices was dedicated in 1924. The building is famous for its murals and other works of art that decorate the halls because of a tax levy that generated almost a million dollars more revenue then was necessary to complete the new statehouse. When the state realized it had all that extra money, officials commissioned some of the most prominent artists of the time to decorate the building. Huge, sweeping murals cover the rotunda ceiling and the hallway walls. They are remarkable for their detail, scope, and variety of artistic styles. They caused controversy as well, with some depicting hard truths about daily life, including the sale of enslaved people and lynching.

The capitol is open to the public and houses the state parks department's history museum, which owns thousands of artifacts featured in multiple ongoing and rotating exhibits.

DIRECTIONS
Return to the North Jefferson trailhead via the bridge and pedestrian/bike bridge. Head east on the trail for about nine miles.

PHOTO COURTESY OF KATHY SCHRENK

Battle of Côte Sans Dessein
MILE MARKER 134

A state parks department plaque marks the spot where a small group of villagers fought off an Indian attack with a combination of skill, ingenuity, and determination, despite being outnumbered nearly 10 to 1.

ILLUSTRATION COURTESY OF
STORIES OF MISSOURI BY JOHN R MUSICK

This settlement, roughly translated to "Coast without Design," was said to be the westernmost permanent European settlement in the United States in 1808. By 1815, about 20 families called the location on the north bank of the Missouri home. On April 4 of that year, the village was attacked by Saux and Fox tribes from the east, despite a treaty signed four months earlier having ended the War of 1812. One of the villagers had spotted an Indian war party approaching the village. All but one of the men in the village went out to meet the attackers. Meanwhile, a group of about 50 natives circled behind the village's fort. The man who had remained behind, with the help of several women who were holed up in the fort, fired at the Indians so quickly, they thought there were several shooters. When the Indians fired flaming arrows at the fort, the women put out the flames with their remaining water, then milk, and then urine captured in bedpans. When the Indians finally retreated, they had lost 14 of their men to the rifleman in the fort.

DIRECTIONS

Head east on the trail. At mile marker 131 is the Tebbetts trailhead and the Turner Katy Trail Shelter, an old building converted into a bunkhouse with running water, electricity, heating, and cooling. The bunks are first come, first served at a cost of $5 per night. Continue east and pass the Mokane trailhead (mile marker 125). Check the state parks website to determine if the trail is open between mile markers 118 and 116. Continue past Bluffton to Rhineland.

PHOTOS COURTESY OF KATHY SCHRENK

4 Rhineland
MILE MARKER 105

In river towns, flooding is a fact of life. The history of the Missouri River hamlets throughout its namesake state is one of give and take, the rising water giving fruitful farmland and taking the structures people dare to place too close to the water's domain. The history books are rife with towns with "new" in front of their names, as well as ones that have stubbornly clung to the edge of the river. Rhineland didn't go so far as to rename itself, but after the Great Flood of 1993, it had had enough. Rhineland was one of the first towns to accept federal funds to move out of a floodplain.

Any midwesterner of a certain age will remember that flood, either from news copter footage of houses floating away or from their own personal experience of living without power or access to the grocery store because of the river coming to their door. In Hermann, the fiscal impact was massive due to a summer and fall with few of the tourists that drive the town's economy. For Rhineland, it meant moving houses and businesses from one side of the Katy to the other. What remains on the river side are ball fields, which are easy enough to repair if another 100-year flood comes along.

PHOTOS COURTESY OF KATHY SCHRENK

FLORA AND FAUNA TO LOOK FOR:
Bald eagles, turkey vultures, rabbits, morning glory, three-toed box turtles, white alder and red alder

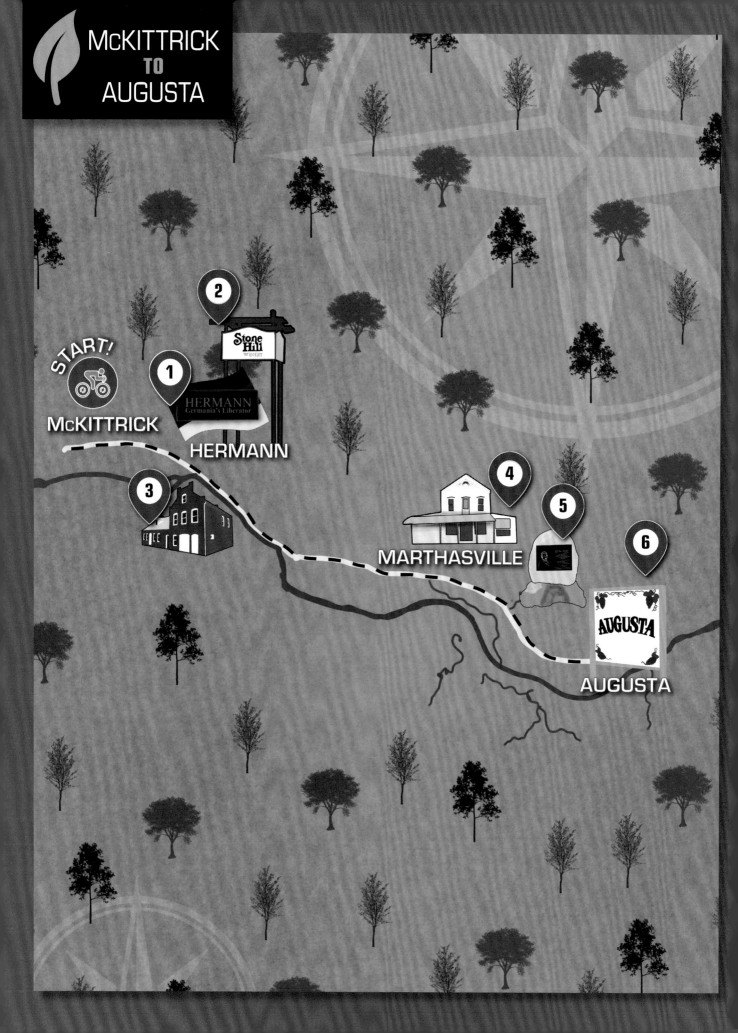

McKITTRICK TO AUGUSTA

START!
McKITTRICK

1 HERMANN

2 Stone Hill WINERY

HERMANN
Germania's Liberator

3

4 MARTHASVILLE

5

6 AUGUSTA

AUGUSTA

RIDE 4

McKITTRICK TO AUGUSTA
34.5 MILES

 ## WHAT TO EXPECT

- Lodging and dining are abundant in Hermann and Augusta.
- Klondike Park has **43** campsites, bathrooms, a fishing lake, and hiking trails.
- Most of the trail is shaded, but there are short sections in full sun so bring sunscreen and sunglasses.
- Water or food may not be available for **10–15** miles east of McKittrick.
- The Peers Store features a clean bathroom, drinks, and snacks for sale.

◤ DIRECTIONS

From Rhineland, head east. Just west of the McKittrick trailhead, take the side trail to the bridge bike lane. Proceed about two miles to Hermann.

① Hermann
2.5 MILES FROM KATY

PHOTO COURTESY OF THE MISSOURI PRESS ASSOCIATION

Hermann was founded in 1837 by German immigrants from Philadelphia. When scouts saw the area that became Hermann, the hills of green and gold rolling along both sides of the Missouri River were reminiscent of the German lands from whence they came, and they had found their new home. By 1847, the settlers had domesticated enough of the area's wild grapevines to start the vineyards that would become Stone Hill Winery. The first precursor to Hermann's wildly popular Oktoberfest was held the following year. In the 1850s, the railroad between St. Louis and Jefferson City made Hermann a stop, adding to its good fortune.

Hermann was booming during the last half of the 19th century and first decade of the 20th, but a tremendous one-two punch—first, the anti-German sentiment of World War I, and then Prohibition—plunged the town into the Depression 10 years ahead of the rest of the world. Though Prohibition ended in 1933, it wasn't until the 1960s that locals revived the wine industry and made tourism the primary economic driver of the town. The town retains its historic quality because many owners couldn't afford to modernize buildings, and a ride or stroll through the streets feels like exploring a huge, living museum. A large swath of the downtown is designated as a national historic district.

 ## DIRECTIONS
From Market Street, follow 8th Street as it heads west and then curves south and turns into Stone Hill Highway.

② Stone Hill Winery
2.5 MILES FROM KATY

For the quintessential Missouri wine-country experience, visit Stone Hill Winery. Set on a hill above town, the views stretch from the 170-year-old buildings that house the tasting room, restaurant, and cellars, down over the carefully tended craggy-shaped vines reaching across their trellises like welcoming arms. At the start of the 20th century, Stone Hill was one of 20 wineries operating in this region and the third-largest in the world. Be sure to take the free winery

PHOTO COURTESY OF STONE HILL WINERY

tour into the wine caves deep below the tasting rooms. The descent into the heart of the historic wine-making operation is like a trip through time. No air-conditioning is needed; it's cool in the summer as a result of being carved deep into the hillside. Hundreds of feet of hand-dug passageways make up the longest continuous wine cellar in North America. The scale and sense of history in the deep, vast underground rooms rival anything in the vaunted wine regions of California's Napa and Sonoma Valleys.

PHOTO COURTESY OF THE STATE HISTORICAL SOCIETY OF MISSOURI

DIRECTIONS
Retrace your route to go down the hill to 2nd and Market Streets.

③ Deutschheim State Historic Site
2.5 MILES FROM KATY

The settlers who founded Hermann were hoping to find a place where they could create a settlement that was German, through and through. When they described Missouri in their mid-1800s writings, they called it Deutschheim, roughly translated as "German Home."

Deutschheim State Historic Site offers tours of historic homes, including the Pommer-Gentner House, which was built in 1840 and is one of the oldest remaining buildings in Hermann. The immigrants who built these houses were part of a wave of German immigration to North America, a result of economic inequality and political upheaval in their home states. Once they arrived in their new home and witnessed neighbors enslaving Africans, they took up that cause and formed one of the central pillars of the abolitionist movement in Missouri.

 DIRECTIONS
Return to the Katy Trail by going back over the bridge via the bike lane. It's about 20 miles to the Peers Store.

④ Peers Store
MILE MARKER 81

Depending on the day, cyclists coming from the west might hear bluegrass coming from the Peers Store before they set eyes on the idyllic 1893 general store building, meticulously restored by the Katy Land Trust. It opened just before the turn of the 20th century as Glosemeyer General Store to soak up some of the dollars flowing to the river corridor in the wake of railroad construction.

The store serves not only as an oasis in a stretch of quiet trail with few places to stop for a snack, but also as a mini museum and a place to buy books and pamphlets on just about any imaginable subject related to local history. Walking over the old porch and across the floorboards feels like a journey through time. Though the goods are different, the sense of community and the feel of the old building are rooted in the era when the place traded in bolts of calico and bulk seed.

 DIRECTIONS
Head east on the Katy. After about five miles, turn left on Boone Memorial Drive, and go about a half mile up the hill to the monument.

5 Daniel Boone Memorial
MILE MARKER 76

Just past Marthasville, next to Lake Creek Winery, is the first burial site of Daniel Boone. That's right, the FIRST burial site. The legendary frontiersman is often associated with taming the wilds of the fledgling United States in environs further east, but just before the turn of the century, he headed west. He died in Missouri near Marthasville in 1820, but years later, boosters of the city of Frankfort, Kentucky, came to Marthasville to reclaim their favorite son, digging up his bones and relocating them to the Kentucky state capital. In the ensuing centuries, historians have debated whether the Frankfortites actually dug up the right body.

? DID YOU KNOW?

The Boone home and historic village is about seven miles by road from the Katy Trail. Buildings from the Boone era have been moved to the village from nearby settlements, recreated by nearby Lindenwood University, which donated the land and buildings to St. Charles County in 2016. The county parks department manages the land and buildings and offers tours.

PHOTO COURTESY OF THE STATE HISTORICAL SOCIETY OF MISSOURI

◀ DIRECTIONS

Augusta is 10 miles east of the Boone Memorial.

6 Augusta
MILE MARKER 66.5

Augusta was founded as Mount Pleasant by one of Daniel Boone's entourage in 1822. It retains much of the same old-world German charm as Hermann and climbs up the hill from the Katy with as much history, quaint architecture, and small-town beauty as any town on the Katy.

Less than half a mile from the trail are the Mount Pleasant Winery and Augusta Winery. Mount Pleasant is the oldest in the Augusta appellation, founded in 1859, and the third largest in the state. Augusta Winery was founded in 1988, making it one of the younger wineries in the state but still a competitor in the same state and national wine competitions as wineries 130 years older.

PHOTO COURTESY OF CARRIE POLK

PHOTO COURTESY OF CURT DENNISON

? DID YOU KNOW?

Augusta is home to the first American Viticultural Area, designated by the federal government in 1980. It was a recognition of the area's long history of wine growing and the unique climate and geography that influence the wines' characteristics.

FLORA AND FAUNA TO LOOK FOR:

Trumpet creeper (look for bright orange blooms in spring), three-toed box turtles , raccoon, wild turkey

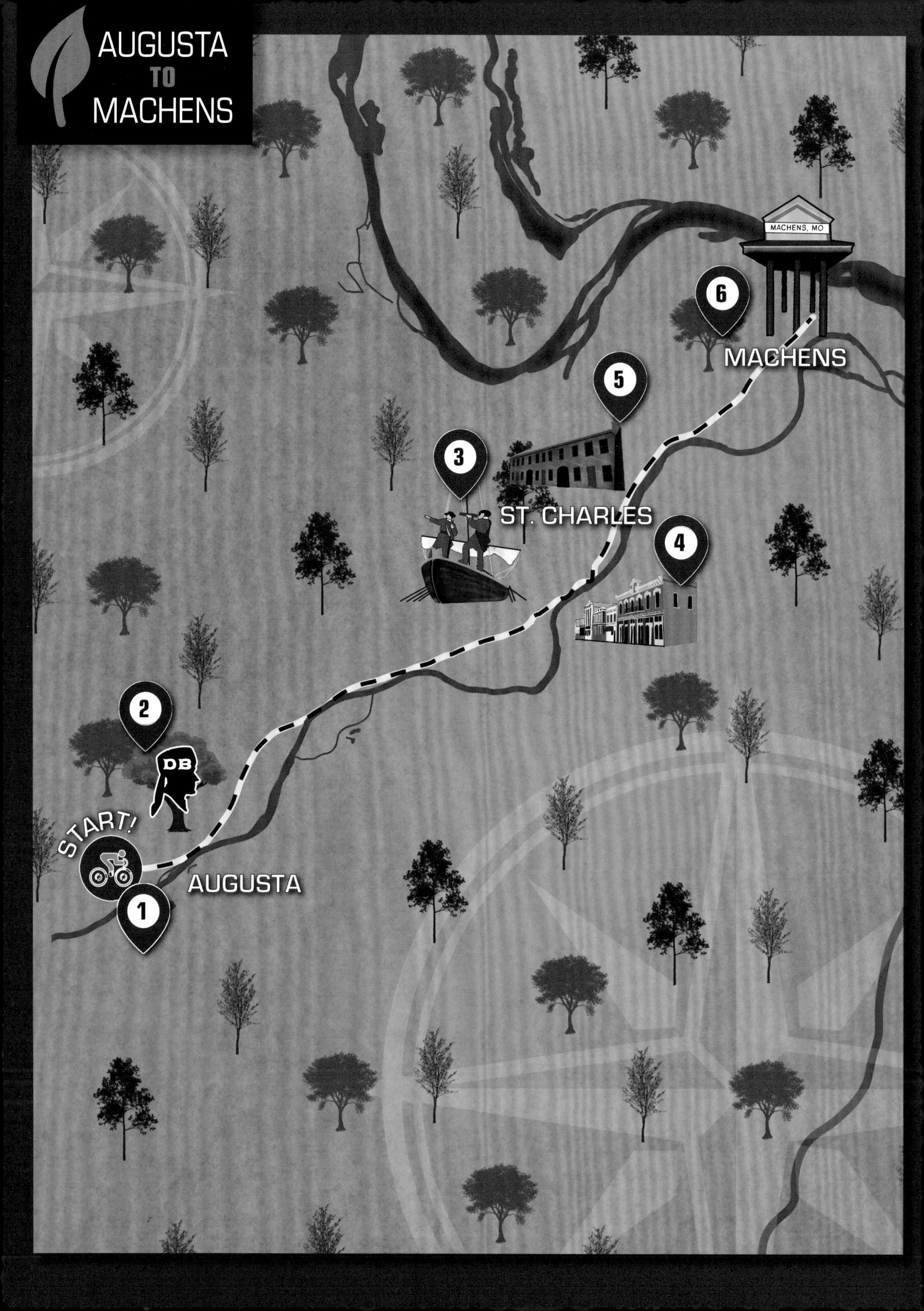
AUGUSTA
TO
MACHENS
MACHENS, MO
MACHENS
ST. CHARLES
START!
DB
AUGUSTA
1
2
3
4
5
6

RIDE 5

AUGUSTA TO MACHENS
39.5 MILES

WHAT TO EXPECT

- There may not be food or water available for 15–20 miles east of Defiance.
- The section of trail between Weldon Springs and St. Charles may be the busiest of the entire trail. Use caution, especially on weekends when the weather is pleasant. Keep to the right-hand side of the trail, and call out when passing.
- Downtown St. Charles has perhaps the highest concentration of lodging, restaurants, and shopping anywhere along the trail, including the Bike Stop Café that is visible from the trail and offers gear, repair services, and cafe food.
- The Katy Trail ends in Machens, but there are no resources besides a pit outlet there—not even a parking lot. The trail unceremoniously ends after 237 miles in Machens, effectively a ghost town, in the narrow, low-lying section of agricultural land between the Missouri and Mississippi Rivers.

DIRECTIONS

Head back to the Katy, and ride east about four miles to the Klondike Park Boat Ramp. Follow signs to take the Lewis & Clark Trail northeast to the hiking trailheads and campsites.

1 Klondike Park
MILE MARKER 64

Klondike Park is one of the best places to experience the wild side of central Missouri. Along the Katy Trail, the trees create a canopy that evokes a sense of being utterly surrounded by nature. Soaring cliffs rise just north of the trail—their mottled patterns of color and texture telling of centuries of wind, rain, flooding, and freezing. The trees begin to disperse as the land slopes down toward the wide Missouri River.

PHOTO COURTESY OF KATHY SCHRENK

Dirt and paved trails crisscross the park, which was transformed from decades as a silica quarry into one of the crown jewels of St. Charles County's rich parks system. Bike parking is available next to the Katy, where one trail heads down to the river through the floodplain and the forests that thrive in the wet soil. Up the hill, paved and dirt trails circle the park and then head straight up the steep hill to the bluff. The bluff view at Klondike is second to none. At the top of the hill, visitors can gaze out over the trees on both sides of the Missouri.

DIRECTIONS
Go about two miles east on the Katy and, just past Lucille Avenue, follow the signs to the Judgment Tree Memorial on the right.

⦿ Daniel Boone Judgement Tree
MILE MARKER 61

PHOTO COURTESY OF THE STATE HISTORICAL SOCIETY OF MISSOURI

The Daniel Boone Judgment Tree Memorial recognizes Boone's standing in the community. He was made a commandant, or syndic, by the Spanish, and held court under a tree near here while mediating disputes that arose among the settlers. A sign displays many photos, documents, and historical writings about Boone and his time here. The signage lauds the volunteers that planted and dedicated the tree in 1999 as a recognition of Boone's enduring impact on the land.

Daniel Boone was famous in his own time as an explorer of what was then the western United States: Pennsylvania and Kentucky. He was 64 years old when he moved his family to Missouri in 1799, after losing their land in Kentucky. He was lured to what is now Missouri Boone Country in part by Spanish authorities, who wanted white settlers in the area and gave Boone 850 acres along Femme Osage Creek, near mile marker 57 on the Katy Trail. This section of trail has been marked by the state parks department with informative signage that vividly describes the explorer's time here. There are few better places to reflect on Boone's legacy and imagine what this region was like 220 years ago.

DIRECTIONS

Head east about 20 miles. Turn right on Riverside Drive, and the Lewis & Clark Boat House and Museum will be on the left.

⦿ Lewis & Clark Boat House and Museum
MILE MARKER 39

PHOTO COURTESY OF KATHY SCHRENK

Everyone has heard of Lewis and Clark, especially in Missouri. Their expedition is one of the reasons St. Louis is called the Gateway City. But St. Charles was the true home base when the 50 or so explorers were preparing to journey into the great unknown of the Louisiana Purchase. The museum has a vast collection of dioramas and memorabilia in a space that looks out over the river itself. During special events, reenactors simulate the expedition's start using life-size replica boats built to look as authentic as possible. These incredible vessels are stored under the museum and are visible to visitors.

DIRECTIONS

From the trail near Frontier Park, take any perpendicular street to access Main Street.

St. Charles's Main Street
MILE MARKER 39

Main Street is a journey through history in itself. The road is paved with uneven bricks, and many buildings facing the street have maintained their historic quality. (If you don't want to ride on the bricks, stick to the Katy or smooth Riverside Drive just a block away, or park your bike at one of the many racks.) The blocks of Main Street between Clark Street and Boone's Lick Road are jammed with shops selling books, clothes, toys, gifts, and art.

PHOTO COURTESY OF THE STATE HISTORICAL SOCIETY OF MISSOURI

DIRECTIONS

Follow Main Street to the block between Madison Street and First Capital Drive.

First State Capital Historic Site
MILE MARKER 39

St. Charles was the first state capital, hosting the legislature in the 1820s, before the state capital was moved to its permanent home in the more central Jefferson City location. St. Charles won the privilege of hosting the first seat of government for the state by offering free meeting space for legislators in second-floor rooms above a general store. The buildings fell into disrepair in the early 20th century, but the state parks department acquired them in 1960. They're restored to resemble the dry goods store and state legislature chambers of 200 years ago.

DIRECTIONS

Return to the trail and enjoy the scenery on the way to Black Walnut. It's a wild mishmash of natural beauty, farmland vistas, and industrial environments. Watch for a lily pond that is magnificently in bloom in late summer, just off the trail near mile marker 31.

DID YOU KNOW?

A five-mile paved trail connects the Katy four miles west of downtown St. Charles to Creve Coeur County Park in St. Louis County. Follow the signs to a separated bike and pedestrian lane on the Veterans Memorial Bridge across the Missouri River.

Before the advent of widespread car ownership after World War II, a streetcar carried St. Louis City residents to this idyllic park. Today, hikers on the Bootleggers Trail on the hill above the lake can see hulking cement remnants of a tram that ferried visitors up and down the hillside. The lake, one of the largest natural lakes in Missouri, was host to rowing events in the 1904 Olympics hosted by St. Louis.

6 Machens
MILE MARKER 26.9

Infamous mountain man Jim Beckwourth spent part of his life in Portage de Sioux, which is a few miles by road from Machens. Beckwourth was born in Virginia around 1800 to an enslaved black woman, making him a slave at birth. His father, his mother's enslaver, moved here when Jim was a boy. Eventually, his father granted young Jim his freedom, and he headed west, joining a fur trapping expedition in 1822. For about 10 years, he lived with the Crow tribe, learning their language and even marrying at least two Crow women.

His adventuresome nature drew him to work as a scout for the US Army and a fur company. Late in his life, he rejoined the Crow tribe, where he died in the 1860s.

? DID YOU KNOW?
The Katy Trail ends at mile marker 26.9 because the Katy Trail uses the same mile numbering system used when the railroad was in service. The MKT rail line stopped here, where trains could make a connection to St. Louis via the Chicago, Burlington, & Quincy Railroad. The section of trail between St. Charles and Machens was the last to open, in 2011.

PHOTO COURTESY OF THE STATE HISTORICAL SOCIETY OF MISSOURI

 FLORA AND FAUNA TO LOOK FOR:
Herons on the Creve Coeur Lake ponds, river otters, garter snakes and lots of frogs east of St. Charles, water lilies

FAMILY OUTINGS
ROCHEPORT, ST. CHARLES, AND JEFFERSON CITY

1 Rocheport
DISTANCE: 10–18 MILES
TIME: 1.5–3 HOURS

Rocheport is on one of the most scenic sections of the trail. This is a good outing for bigger kids who can ride for 10 miles or more, and kids in trailers or on a third-wheel attachment behind an adult.

Start your ride at the Rocheport trailhead. Head west just half a mile to the 243-foot-long arched Rocheport tunnel, the only one on the Katy Trail, which was built on the MKT line at Rocheport around 1893. Travel through the tunnel and toward the west to check out the inside of the tunnel and the surrounding cliffs. On the way back to town, check out a short hiking trail on the right, near a wayside maker, for a lovely, secluded view of the river in the Diana Bend Conservation Area.

Enjoy the scenery of the river as your constant companion on the right and the soaring cliffs on the left. At mile marker 177.5, you'll notice a doorway around a man-made wall of rocks. This was an explosives storage bunker used by workers when the railroad was under construction in the 19th century.

About three miles west, Lewis and Clark Cave is visible right next to the trail. Heed the signs warning against trespassing in the cave. Then, look up and to the left to try to spot the native drawings on the rock. These images predate European exploration. Ask your kids why they think indigenous people would have drawn these images.

If you turn around here, your trip will be about 10 miles total. Keep going along this scenic stretch another five miles to turn right on Bur Oak Road and see the big Bur Oak. This is one of the largest such oaks in the country and is regionally beloved for its picturesque place in the midst of a field with no other trees around.

For a longer adventure, continue east and then north on a trail connecting to Columbia. Turning around at the Bur Oak results in a round trip of about 18 miles. Once back at the trailhead, you'll find a handful of restaurants in Rocheport that would make a good post-ride meal.

PHOTO COURTESY OF THE STATE HISTORICAL SOCIETY OF MISSOURI

PHOTO COURTESY OF KATHY SCHRENK

PHOTO COURTESY OF DAN BURKHARDT

② St. Charles
DISTANCE: 5–25 MILES
TIME: 1–3 HOURS

St. Charles is crammed full of things to do and see. Start your adventure at the St. Charles trailhead parking at the southwest end of the downtown historic district. Here, the Lewis & Clark Boat House and Museum offer fascinating exhibits for kids of all ages. Even if you don't go in to the museum, climb the steps to the platform and take in the full-size replicas of boats that Lewis and Clark's crew would have rowed.

PHOTO COURTESY OF THE STATE HISTORICAL SOCIETY OF MISSOURI

Ride northeast on the trail just a mile or two to take in the historic downtown St. Charles district and Frontier Park. You'll find more museums, lots of shops—including bike shops and a bookstore—restaurants, and coffee shops. Keep pedaling another mile or so, and the scenery becomes distinctly industrial. The trail borders a junkyard with ruined cars stacked four or five high. Continue another mile or so, and the view changes again, this time to rural scenery of riverside bluffs, tunnels created by trailside trees, and farmland. A few miles past St. Charles, these views continue all the way to Machens. At the Katy Trail's unceremonious end after 237 miles, the scene is eerily quiet, unless a train is passing on the line that is still in use and had once served as a connection to St. Louis for trains that plied the MKT rails.

PHOTO COURTESY OF THE LIBRARY OF CONGRESS

3 Jefferson City

DISTANCE: SIX MILES
TIME: 1–3 HOURS

The North Jefferson Katy trailhead is just over the Missouri River from the state capital and its attendant views, museums, and art.

Though a short ride, this is better for kids who have some experience riding on streets.

Take the spur trail from the parking lot and head southwest. This path can get muddy, so use Katy Road as an alternative if necessary. Stay on the Katy Spur as it passes under Highway 94 and then turn right on 4th Street. Turn left on Cottonwood Street, which leads to the pedestrian-bike ramp to the Jefferson City Bridge.

The ramp itself is a sight to see, basically a series of shorter ramps looping around to allow access to the dedicated bike lane on the southeast side of the bridge. The lane leads trail users to the intersection of Clay and West Main streets. From here, take in the view down Main Street toward the capitol. It's one of the last statehouses constructed in this Roman renaissance style, similar to the US Capitol Building in Washington, DC.

Ride down Main Street about half a mile to circle the building, which includes the parks department's state history museum. The halls of the capitol are open to the public for tours (check the parks website for details) where visitors can see world-class works of art (for more on the Capitol artwork, see page 13).

The capitol building is surrounded by memorials to veterans, law enforcement, and Lewis and Clark, as well as gardens and historic buildings. Don't miss the view of the river from the circular drive in front of the capitol. Just south of the capitol are plenty of places to find food before the ride back to the trailhead.

PHOTO COURTESY OF STATE HISTORICAL SOCIETY OF MISSOURI

WINERY
RAMBLE

7  LOST CREEK

6  Holy Grail

4 Blumenhof WINERY

2 MOUNT PLEASANT WINERY

START!

1 SUGAR CREEK WINERY

DEFIANCE

MARTHASVILLE

5 LAKE CREEK WINERY

DUTZOW

AUGUSTA

MATSON

3 AUGUSTA WINERY

RIDE 9

WINERY RAMBLE
AUGUSTA AREA

Augusta Area Winery Tour
DISTANCE: 30–40 MILES
TIME: 2 DAYS

Missouri boasts one of the oldest wine-growing regions in the country, and the Katy Trail is tailor-made for touring the vineyards and tasting rooms. Most of these wineries are a stone's throw from the trail. Detours of a few miles could take adventurous oenophiles to a dozen more. While pedaling through the Missouri River bottomlands, one can easily imagine the first German settlers in the 1800s gazing up at the rolling hillsides and making the connection with their homeland. It's no coincidence that the Missouri wines you taste here have much in common with the Rieslings and Gewurztraminers of the central European appellations.

Start your trip with an overnight stay at a bed-and-breakfast in Augusta or Defiance, or choose a campsite in Klondike Park just east of Augusta.

Near mile marker 62 just above the Matson trailhead is **Sugar Creek Winery (1)**. Head up the hill on Boone Country Lane—it's close enough to push your bike up the steep grade if need be. You'll enjoy indoor and outdoor tasting in this family-run business atmosphere. It's often quiet here, but even on busy weekends, you'll have plenty of room to spread out as you sip.

Augusta (mile marker 66) feels like a bustling city compared to some of the towns along the wine trail—but in a good way. At least two wineries in Augusta are worth a stop and well within easy walking distance from the Katy Trail. **Mount Pleasant Winery (2)** is one of the biggest wineries in the area and one of the busiest. It's got a huge tasting room, sprawling patio, and gorgeous views of the valley. Live music on the weekends makes for a party atmosphere. **Augusta Winery (3)** is in the heart of Augusta and has a more intimate tasting room with a quiet view of the street and other historic buildings.

Blumenhof Vineyards and Winery (4) is just a half mile from the Katy Trail on a stretch of Highway 94 where the traffic slows to go through the little town of Dutzow. Near mile marker 74, turn on to Highway 94 and head up the hill. The right turn into the Blumenhof parking lot could be mistaken for a trip to a winery in the heart of Germany, with the tasting room's Bavarian architecture and vines rolling away to the horizon.

Marthasville (5) is great place to stop for the night during your wine tour. Myriad bed-and-breakfasts and camping spots are available to choose from.

Just east of the trailhead, you'll hear **Lake Creek Winery (5)**. That's right, hear. On weekends, just follow the sound of the live music up the hill to the tasting room and the spacious patio. It's just a quarter mile from the trail on Boone Monument Road near mile marker 76.

From Treloar (mile marker 85), head about 1.5 miles up Highway N to **Holy Grail Winery (6)**. This small winery is a contrast to many of the wineries in the region with its use of grapes from other regions. Some of its wines are more similar to California reds than the Nortons and Chambourcins typical in Missouri wines.

One of the best things about **Lost Creek Winery (7)** is the feeling that you might be lost as you make your way up the gravel road to the vineyard, although there's actually little chance of this because it's only a third of a mile up the hill from the trail near mile marker 94 on Gore Road. The vibe here is as much farmhouse as tasting room.

INDEX